SILENT GIFTS

dedicated to all who long for a better world,
mentally, physically and environmentally.

Published by Rural Arts. November, 2020
Great Britain
Copyright © 2020 All rights reserved

Printed by 'All Things Print'

This book offers an insight into the plants that you may find, or you can grow in your back garden. It reflects their uses, the wildlife that they attract, the remedies that they can give and the folklore, myths and stories that have been passed down through generations.

The Celtic tree calendar follows the 13 cycles of the moon through the year. It is intriguing and linked to your date of birth, reflects your personality traits.

I invite you to plant a tree for your descendants on your birthday, every year.

Your garden is a salvation; plant for the birds, plant for the animals, plant for the insects. Look after your plants and their silent gifts will look after your mental and physical health and the health of our planet.

Live simply, be extraordinary.

Thank you.

CONTENTS

The Birch *Betula Pendula*

Gifts
Birch is the first tree to grow in a wood after fire. It is known for symbolising a fresh start, a new beginning.

This hardwood is used to make beautiful light-coloured furniture; it is easily turned for making spools, reels, wooden toys, etc. Twisted dried bark can be used instead of candles as it is very flammable and small pieces of bark make excellent firelighters, wet or dry.

Remedies
The birch bark contains Betulin; this profoundly helps in acting as a treatment for skin conditions such as shingles, eczema and burns, often more effective than conventional treatment. Sap can make a soothing tea. The twigs bunched together are for beating oneself to increase healthy blood circulation during a sauna perhaps!

Wildlife
334 different species of insects have been identified living on the birch tree including ladybirds and moths such as the wonderfully named buff tip and pebble hooktip. The caterpillars of the moths eat the new spring shoots; the chaffinches, robins and tree pipet eat the caterpillars. In the autumn other birds come to eat the seeds such as siskin and greenfinch.

Folklore and Myth
So many myths about the Birch tree: The baby who is laid in a cradle made of birch is protected from evil spirits. The birch twig besom was used to brush clean the floor especially in the New Year sweeping out the old. Birch switches were used to beat wicked spirits out of children, prisoners, and lunatics. It symbolises meekness and new beginnings.

Celtic Birth Sign: Late December through January
These folk are driven with ambition. They are motivated to improve life and have high ideals, often leaders in their field. They encourage others and make new beginnings possible. Socially, they brighten a gathering with their charm.

The First Tree
The first tree, the nymph,
Pushing through the tangled detritus on the
forest floor.
The mesmeric moon reflects on silvered branches.
New ideas shimmer white and soon
Become fulfilled and dreams bloom.

Nettles *Urtica dioica*

Gifts
During the First World War, Germany suffered a shortage of cotton and nettles were used to produce German army uniforms. The nettle string is strong and easily made by stripping off the leaves and soaking in water over night. Take out the pith by splitting the stem. Split the outside of the nettle nettle into two and start to twist, there are many ways of doing this. One is to twist the stems in a clockwise direction with both hands. One on each stem. Another is to roll the string on your thigh. Add other lengths through laying on other pieces as you go.

Remedies
Nettles have been known to help with rheumatism. Giving yourself a good flogging with nettles apparently helps! They have been used to ease urinary infections and prostate problems. The leaves can be placed on your skin to help with aching muscles.

Use dried leaves for a tea to treat pain, osteoarthritis, allergies and hay fever. The root will help eczema and hair loss. Make wonderful soup as after a long winter, the fresh young leaves are full of iron and will boost the oxygen in your body and that feeds your hymoglobin and muscle cells.

Wild Life
Forty species of insects enjoy living amongst the nettle, the stings protecting them from grazing animals. The caterpillars of the small tortoiseshell and peacock butterflies use the nettle as food in the spring. Ladybirds feast on the aphids that shelter along the spiky stems. The birds enjoy the caterpillars and insects in the spring and in the autumn the enormous amount of seeds that nettles produce.

Folklore and Myth   *The element of fire.*
Milarepa, a Buddhist saint, had his fortune stolen by his Aunt and Uncle. After this, his family had to live in poverty. Milarepa took revenge, using magic to wreak havoc on a wedding and ruining their crops with hailstones. But, he then felt guilty and went to live in a cave where he ate nothing but nettles. After many years, he turned green and hairy. He is now known as the Green God.

In Norse mythology, Loki the mischievous and shape-changer God made a net out of nettles to catch fish. He threw the net on a fire when he saw the other Gods searching for him. He changed himself into a salmon and jumped into the river, the burnt net was seen by the other Gods and another was made to catch him. It was then that he decided to swim upstream, leaping up water-falls, to escape capture.

Hans Christian Anderson wrote a beautiful story called 'The Wild Swans'. in it a princess had to make seven coats out of nettles for her brothers who had been turned into swans by a witch. The princess had to pick the nettles without making a sound or noticing the pain and weave the coats to fling onto their backs in order to break the spell.

Turn towards the sun
Eyes closed drinking long lost light,
Warming winter bones

Stinging Nettle Soup:

Collect your young nettles in thick gardening gloves. Wash and tear off the leaves and discard the stalks.

Gently sweat an onion and one garlic bulb in olive oil or 2oz butter, till soft, add them to a pot containing a litre of stock, one carrot and one potato and cook gently for 15 minutes. Add the leaves for a further 10 mins. Puree, then swirl creme fraiche on the top. You have a soup which certainly does you good and has an elegant smokey flavour.

The Rowan *Sorbus aucuparia*

Gifts

The rowan can be seen growing more commonly in Northern Europe. It grows happily in mountainous regions, on stoney ground that is inhospitable to deer and sheep who would eat the young saplings. The timber can be used for tool handles and was the chosen wood for spinning wheels. Rowan can be carved and makes excellent walking sticks. The bark was used in the tanning process. Try divining with rowan for metal objects.

The berries, leaves and sap are toxic; however, cooking the berries will change the chemistry and so they become edible. The cooked berries make wonderful jelly, sauces and wine.

Wildlife

In spring, rowan blossom attracts pollinating insects. Every two or three years the rowan masts, that is, it produces a bumper crop of berries. This is in defence against the rowan moth, more commonly known as the apple fruit moth that consumes the berries in autumn. The berries are also a feast for numerous birds in particular the thrushes, the blackbirds and the redstarts.

Folklore and Myth

Many stories exist about the rowan. In Greek mythology, Hebe had carelessly lost the ambrosia cup to demons. The gods sent an eagle to retrieve it. There was a fight and where the feathers and drops of blood landed on the ground a rowan tree grew. The leaves of the rowan look very like the eagles feathers and the berries the drops of blood.

It was said to never cut a rowan with a knife; instead a branch can be pulled off and used for carving or making into a small cross and tied together with red thread. These were charms carried in pockets for protection, also worn by cattle and hung in the home from lintels.

The Celtic Birth Sign: January through February

Born in the time of the Rowan, you are very sympathetic to others and are a great asset with your creative thoughts and ideals. You have a philosophy that enables you to become influential, although you can be thought of as rather aloof at times and can be misunderstood. Others can always rely on you however, to come up with very different points of view.

Light and promise dawns
from the deep velvet quiet
where the Rowan grows.

9

Gorse *Ulex*

Gifts
Gorse gives that wonderful scent of musky coconut that comes in the spring from the vivid yellow flower that produces a yellow dye for painting or dying, The spikes are sharp so the bush, when planted in a hedge, helps to make it stock proof. The branches were once used for sweeping chimneys and stables. They were also laid in streams to collect precious gold dust as it adheres to the plant.

Wildlife
The bright yellow flowers beckon to the bees who gratefully come to gather nectar, pollinating as they go. Gorse attracts many birds such as the linnet, the yellowhammer, and the dartford warbler. They feed on insects that live on the flowers and in autumn on the seed pods that crackle as they split. Birds love to use the gorse as shelter from extreme weather as it is very dense. It has good nutritional value as forage for goats and other livestock.

Remedies
The leaf buds can be used for a tea infusion; add some honey and enjoy the delicate aroma and deliciously refreshing taste. It is known to bring light where there is darkness, to change hopeless feelings into positive thought. The gorse gives hope and the symbolism given to those of intelligence who look at the gorse and breathe its scent tells them how everything will come right.

Symbolism   *Embodies hope*
Energy, independence, intelligence, industry. Encourages those who are born in the spring to do something because it feels right because it makes sense. It is said 'When gorse is out of bloom, kissing is out of season'. Luckily the gorse is always in bloom somewhere.

Yellow blaze from spiky bower
Musky smell, the kissing flower.

The Ash *Fraxinus*

Gifts
The ash is a durable and long-lasting hardwood that is ideal for tools and handles. It is used to make tillers for narrow boats and is one of the woods used for coffins. The 'Morgan' car company still makes the wood frames out of ash, now treated to stop any rot.

A 400-year-old coppiced ash tree can still provide wood for charcoal. You can use the wood for your winter fire and, rather like oak, it burns for a long time throwing out a good heat.

Remedies
If you want to try using ash as a medicine for ills including gout and earache, kidney stones and warts, try boiling bark pieces for 20 minutes and drink 2 or 3 times a day. This is not proven science but is considered a traditional medicine. If you like capers, you might try and pickle the young green seeds.

Wildlife
Light penetrates through the wide-spaced branches allowing flora to grow beneath. The holes in the trunk and branches make a good habitat for birds such as owls and bats A good tree to find squirrel dreys and woodland birds nests. The ash tree is home to insects and moths. The larvae of the Tawny Pinion moth feeds mostly on the ash tree.

The ash trees are being attacked and sometimes destroyed by ash die back caused by the fungus (*Hymenoscyphus fraxineus*) This originated in eastern asia. Once weakened by the die back the tree can succumb to honey fungus and this can then competely kill the tree.

Celtic Birth Sign: February through March
Astrology considers those born during this period to be artistic, creative, freethinkers, often working through their intuition. Sometimes thought of as being moody, they are inspired with nature, poetry and art. Their interests also lie in science and theology. A charming personality.

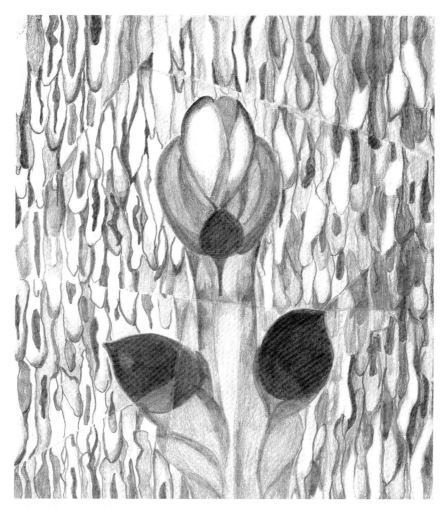

Folklore and Myth

The growth of this tree can reach 200'. This reflects the celtic meaning: the more you attain the more important it is for you to stay grounded. It was considered that the realm of the earth and the sky were held together by the mighty ash. It has always been thought of as the protector of children. No grief for a child with a spoonful of sap.

Leaves in the cradle stop mysterious forces from turning your child to a changeling. Druids carry a staff of ash, symbolizing the connection between the earth and the sky. Five trees guard Ireland, three of these are ash trees, planted near holy wells and sacred springs. Harm the tree at your peril, as this could release unearthly events and magic.

The Larch *Larix*

Gifts
Larch is one of the very few conifers that loses its needles in the autumn. A beautiful tree with soft delicate fronds. It is strong and hardens over time and therefore extremely useful. This timber is used for cladding houses, boat building, telegraph poles and many other commercial purposes as it is not affected by damp, or rot; excellent for railway sleepers. It is a fast growing tree compared to the oak and is therefore much sought-after and valued.

Remedies
Peel off some of the bark and take off the outer layer. What you are left with can be used to make an expectorant for chronic bronchitis. Externally this can also be used as a relief for eczema, psoriasis and as a disinfectant. It can be taken as a a treatment for cystitis.

Wild Life
If you are lucky enough to have red squirrels near you, they eat the young seeds of the tree as do the siskin and redpolls. The long-eared owl enjoys the protection of this tree and magpies can choose the larch to make a nest.

Folklore and Myth
If you want to ward off evil spirits then burn some larch wood on your fire as the smoke will keep them away. Or, you can make a charm out of the twigs or a slice of a small branch and design a pendant to ward off the evil eye.
Plant a larch in your garden in memory of a loved one. The soft gentle fronds of the tree will contain their spirit, always guarding and looking after you. A Siberian world tree taking the place of the ash.

Magpies

Exited magpies
Choose a larch to build their nest.
One stick, then another,
Strength testing and twig tangling
Five days, tirelessly.
Sixth day they rest and fearlessly
Balance on this messy platform to
Produce their young.

The Alder *Alnus*

Gifts
The alder is found growing on the banks of rivers and lakes. It has the gift of becoming hard when immersed in water over long periods. It is therefore used in situations that require timber to remain strong when in water such as locks, troughs and boats. Venice was built using piles made of alder timber. Those who were working underground in mines, where there was often water lying, were given clogs made of alder to wear.

The charcoal of the alder is used to smoke fish. The black cracked bark gives a red dye and the leaves produce a strong green and the twigs a useful brown. It is also used to make gunpowder. The alder does not split when nailed. The tree provides its own nitrogen and will improve the soil where it is planted.

Wildlife
The alder attracts insects and in the autumn siskins and gold finches particularly love to visit and feast on the alder seeds.

Remedies
Warm a bag of alder leaves
To help calm itchy skin
Leave some in your shoes
Sore feet revive therein

Boil up bark and gargle
Tonsillitis finds relief.
Helps with ulcers in the mouth,
Stops you feeling grief.

Celtic Birth Sign: March through April
Those born in this time are like the phoenix, rebuilding themselves after each defeat or setback. They have the gift of wisdom and vigour, giving aid in academic and business ventures. They make great orators and have strength and courage blended with generosity of spirit and compassion.

Folklore and Myth

The elements fire and water

In Ireland it was thought to bring you bad luck if your travels brought you near an alder wood, probably because their roots love boggy ground and the evil spirits that lurk in the bog could pull you in and keep you there. Never cut an alder tree as the sap is blood red and this can upset all the fairies that live within.

The three-headed serpent Greek God Cronus was considered to represent time. The alder tree was sacred to this god because it was thought to be the tree of knowledge for past, present and future.

Narrow Leaf Plantain Weed   *Plantago lanceolata*

Gifts
Discovering plantain is rather similar to finding a precious book amongst a pile in a charity shop, overlooked and yet it offers such gifts for us. A plant that we are most likely to walk over every day. Sometimes called a toe knocker because as you stride across land where there are many plantains growing they knock your feet with their seed heads.

Recipes and Remedies
You are out for a country walk and you get stung by a nettle or bee, scratched by brambles and find you have insect bites. Crushing the leaves of the humble plantain and rubbing the juice onto the skin will have much more effect in alleviating the sting and calming the skin than turning to the dock leaf.

If you get a splinter, smash plantain up into a mush and place it on the spot, cover with a plaster overnight and the next morning it will come out easily with a little squeeze.

Making your own ointments and creams: Infuse fresh plantain leaves into coconut oil, olive oil or sweet almond oil. Make certain that the oil covers the leaves, then place a cloth over the top so that it can breathe. Leave in a dark place for four to six weeks. Add to melted beeswax very slowly in a bain-marie. Stir gently and then put into jars. Use this on yourself and your pets to calm irritated or sunburnt skin.

The young leaves are edible and tasty in salads. This plant contains good compounds that promote healing and are anti-inflammatory. The leaves are said to slow your digestive system down but the seeds are a natural laxative. As a tea it can soothe and heal mouth ulcers.

Although plantain is considered a safe and beneficial herb, care must be taken with any herbal remedy in case of an allergic reaction, so always begin with a small amount.

The benefits of calming stomach ulcers and increasing the speed of wound healing have been proven, though again be aware as each of us responds differently.

Wildlife
The goldfinches and sparrows enjoy the seeds of various garden plants and that includes plantain. This plant can produce between 14,000-30,000 seeds every year. A great food source for the birds.

Folklore and Myth   *The element water*
Wind the stem and pop the seed head off; it is used as a catapult to see who can make the seed head go the furthest. 'Miss Molly had a dolly, but her head popped off' Folklore Society, London, June 2010.

Garlic *scorodon or stinking rose.*

Gifts

Celebrate garlic day on April 19th. You had better ask all your friends and family at the same time as the breath problem can be quite extreme. Garlic is good for us and packed with flavour. You can not only eat the bulb, but also on the hard-neck varieties of garlic, the shoots called scapes; the young green shoots are perfect for adding to soups and pestos.

The pyramid builders were given beer, flatbread, raw garlic and onions. When they complained that this was not enough they were given more garlic. This they thought would ward off illnesses.

Remedies

We all eat garlic; on average over 300 cloves per person per year! It keeps the cholesterol down and cures colds (only when eaten raw, absolutely delicious crushed on toast with a sprinkling of olive oil).

Garlic is a natural antibiotic and anti-fungal plant inhibiting enzymes from growing in liver cells. It relaxes the blood vessels, reducing high blood pressure thus is excellent for the heart. The bulbs contain many of the minerals that we need to be healthy and it tastes good.

Slice it and rub it on cold sores and acne; it will speed up the healing. Also, rub onto serious wounds to heal when drug-resistant bacteria are present. Garlic was used for thousands of years before antibiotics took over. Perhaps we should now reverse the process and go back to relying on garlic.

It is said that treating animals with garlic, who are infested with ticks, has been shown to kill the ticks in 30 minutes. I wonder, how do you treat an animal with garlic?

Garlic is also thought to bind with heavy metals and aids in eliminating them from your body.

Folklore and Myth

The Greeks would consume garlic before going into battle. Garlic was supposed to ward off evil spirits causing them to lose their way. In central Europe, garlic was hung in birthing rooms and outside front doors for the same reason.

In Wales there is a saying: Eat leeks in March and garlic in May, then the rest of the year, your doctor can play.

So let's celebrate!

The Willow *Saille*

Gifts
There are 12 main types of willow but hundreds of different varieties. The 'Black Maul' *Salix triandra* is commonly used for basket making. The technique of weaving willow into baskets is an old tradition for purposes such as making cradles, for collecting your harvest, for shopping and for coffins and garden structures. Cricket bats are made from common or white willow with its straight stem and springy properties.

Remedies
Aspirin is made from the willow bark. To make your own natural painkiller, dry the bark and break into small pieces. Brew a tea and drink for a painkiller that is kind to your stomach and liver.

Wildlife
The goat willow or pussy willow attracts the hawk moth's caterpillars who enjoy the young leaves. The aphids that feed on the bark sap produce a sticky substance which drips down and is attractive to wasps and other insects. Deer eat the leaves of willow and so do rabbits.

Folklore and Myth   Tree of Enchantment   *The element water*
The willow is considered to be the first tree just as Adam was the first man. In Druid times it was thought the world and the sun were formed from two red eggs. These eggs were hidden in a willow tree. Now we hide our Easter eggs for children to find symbolising perhaps a new beginning, or rebirth.

After the First World War Monet painted weeping willows in ten paintings to represent the loss and tragedy of all those men lost in battle. There is also a feeling of hope as the renewed strength comes from the central growth of the tree.

Celtic Birth Sign: April through May
Those born in these months are considered to be mysterious and often moody but with a great sense of adventure; with a good memory they succeed in whatever they do. Listening to the inner wisdom rather than taking advice from others. They are remarkably patient and well grounded.

Drops fall from willow wands,
Ripples pattern the water.

Strawberry   Rosaceae family

Gifts
Related to the rose, the strawberry is potently romantic. Pure white blossoms anticipate the juicy, red fruit to follow. Strawberries stop us in our tracks; we bend down to pick and share; love is in the air.

```
        My first strawberry.
My mouth bursts with warm sweet wet sunshine.
        My garden awakes.
```

The strawberry looks after her children; throwing out her young on long, supportive runners, to plant their own feet within the warm earth, beginning anew.

Remedy

The dried leaves of the strawberry plant can be used to make a weak tea - this is nature's toothpaste. It removes stains on teeth, dissolves plaque and refreshes the breath.

Folklore and Myth

This fruit, beloved of goddesses, energised fertility. Strawberries decorating a pregnant cow would ensure a healthy calf. In European folklore, it was said that if a pregnant woman carried strawberry leaves in her pocket this would lessen the pains of childbirth.

In Norse mythology, the spirits of young children on their way to heaven are protected inside the Goddess Frigga's strawberries. Medieval stonemasons carved the perfection of the strawberry on cathedrals and churches, symbolising innocence, purity and humbleness of those who shake off sin as no matter where they are, they lead a life of righteousness. Your life, and the strawberry, when together, hold the future. It portends a new positive beginning for your projects.

The strawberry is found in medieval art representing earthly food for the delight of man kind. It was thought to be a cure for depression.

There are so many artists that choose to place strawberries in their paintings. From Hieronymus Bosch to Marc Chagall to the modern day. Each artist having no doubt there own reasons for placing the humble strawberry in such a significant place in their works.

Picking and eating strawberries brings smiles. Beware sharing a double berry as love will follow!

Riddle from Lithuania

A young lady is standing, wearing a pretty hat;
Whoever walks past her, bows their head low.

The Hawthorn Huath

Gifts
This thorny tree is an effective hedging plant. In May, the hawthorn is covered in pinky-white flowers, as if preparing for a wedding. David Hockney said "It looks as though champagne is being poured over the bushes." He made a stained-glass window for Westminster Abbey including a representation of the hawthorn.

Remedies and Recipes
The berries are anti-inflammatory and full of antioxidants with many health benefits including skin anti-aging. They may also lower blood pressure. Important: Please seek your doctor's advice.

The young leaves and flower buds can be added to salads; the berries turned into jelly or added to chutneys as a flavoursome extra.

Wildlife
This tree provides good nesting sites when grown in hedgerows. It is beloved by 300 insect species. In Autumn, berries feed dormice and many resident bird species as well as winter visiting fieldfares and redwings.

Folklore and Myth   *The element fire*
According to Irish legend, all hawthorns are home to the fairies. A lot of superstition has grown up around this tree. The famous Holy Thorn of Glastonbury flowers twice a year. Originally thought to have been brought to Wearyall Hill by Jesus's uncle, Joseph of Arimathea.

Celtic Birth Sign: May through June
Those born at this time of the year are not what they appear to be. They are seemingly average outside, disguising the passions and creativity that burn within. They have a good sense of humour and are able to comfort others. They appear to be contented people and are excellent listeners.

Joseph's staff struck the ground and there I
grew
To bring the fairies fluttering gaze
Before the guests who seek my fruit
Land and tread on thorny branch
Eat their fill and fly to spill my seed
On fertile soil and there, born again,
I shelter sheep from wind and driving rain

27

Rosemary *Rosmarinus officinalis*

Gifts
Rosemary is a delightful herb that emanates a strong scent, which promotes a sense of sunshine and the Mediterranean countryside. The blue, pinkie, purple flowers in the spring are striking and lift the spirits after the winter. An excellent plant to grow in the garden with its evergreen needle leaves.

Remedies and Recipes
A herb that gives health benefits from lifting your mood to improving memory. An anti-inflammatory herb, it is full of anti-oxidants and a source of calcium and iron. It relieves tension and is excellent for your eyes and your senses.

A perfect accompaniment to lamb or if you are a vegetarian roasted root vegetables.

Wildlife
The early flowers provide much-needed sustenance for emerging bees.

Folklore and Myth   *The elements of air and fire*
Rosemary given to your lover represents faithfulness. Rosemary in your wedding bouquet symbolises love, steadfastness and loyalty.
Call your child Rosemary and you are giving her the names Rose and Mary, together a symbol of remembrance.

Shakespeare had an understanding of
medicinal herbs:

'There's Rosemary, that's for remembrance;
pray, love, remember.'
                    Ophelia, in 'Hamlet'

What was that I saw behind my rosemary bush?
Black, rat size but with no tail
Fast, gone now,
breeding under the back step!

Mint   *mentha*

Gifts

The wonderful aroma of summer with wild mint catching in your breath as you walk on the hillsides, bruising and treading the leaves underfoot. Although mint growing wild is quite rare today, it is possible to find it growing on chalk down in southern England.

There are 12 common edible types of mint and each one has a different flavour. It is a very invasive plant so if you want to grow this herb make sure it is contained. Try a pot without a bottom sunk into the ground.

Remedies

Peppermint is an amazing herb that helps us in so many ways. It freshens breath and is antiseptic, antibacterial and anti-inflammatory. Relieving coughing and congestion in your throat and lungs; excellent for asthmatics and those with breathing problems. Peppermint is also good for headaches and nausea. It aids digestion and sorts out gas and tummy upsets. It also significantly helps with memory retention.

Recipe

Make a face mask out of mint leaves and honey - leave for 20 minutes before rinsing off and notice the subtle change to fresh soft skin.

Awaken your taste buds to the double flavour of mint leaves in a glass of Pimms

Using mint in your cooking is delicious as it goes with so many dishes particularly lamb and many vegetarian recipes.

Then there is chocolate mint. You can dry the mint in bundles and use it to make a delicious tea, or add to iced tea. Try freezing mint leaves in an ice cube and add them to your drinks. Use your mixer to make mint sugar with a bundle of mint and a cup of sugar. Grind together and spread on bread. Try adding apple mint to fruit salads and with your soft cheese - delicious.

Folklore and Myth

The element of air

As always there is lot going on in the Greek myths. Hades was lonely one spring as his wife Persephone left him for sixth months of the year to help her mother the Goddess Ceres. He met Minthe a Nyad and they fell in love. When Persephone became alerted to this, she took her revenge and turned Minthe into a plant. Mint is often associated with death and funerals as it was found in the Egyptian tombs and in stories connected with death.

Often crowns were made of mint; they were called crowns of Venus. Mint was thought to be an aphrodisiac as it disguised wine odours and encouraged love.

There are many forms of use for the word mint. In mint condition, means new and fresh. In Newcastle the word mint is used when some young people have been out on the town and they say ' It was mint' meaning that it was brilliant, fun and enjoyable. To mint coins is to make new coins. Everything connected with mint seems to be fresh and new.

```
Calming hues, mint blue,
Brush and finger feeling their way
Across the canvass blessed
With creating garden fresh view.
```

Rose Bay Willow Herb *Chamerion angustifolium*

Gifts
Fireweed grows on disturbed ground such as railway embankments or land that has been cleared by fires. A tall herb that can grow to 1.20 cm high.

Remedies
It is used for pain and swelling (inflammation), fevers, tumours, wounds, and enlarged prostate (benign prostatic hyperplasia, BPH). It is also used as an astringent and as a tonic.

Pick the young leaves and immature buds for your salad, or steam the shoots as asparagus. Harvest the roots in early spring or late autumn and the flowers in early summer.

Wildlife
The Bedstraw hawk-moth *Hyles gallii* can be found feeding on rosebay willow herb. They are not common in this country because of the rainfall; however you maybe lucky enough to spot the caterpillars that have a red horn above their heads, very impressive.

Folklore and Myth
This plant lights the way for elves. They hide amongst the tall fronds, waiting for unsuspecting intruders. Before you pick any part of the plant ask the permission of the elves to do so. If you don't a thunder storm will follow.

It has been said that each rosebay willow herb that grows on fired earth, symbolises the heart of each scorched tree.


```
            Gentle purple spears
          From fired earth grows
      From the graves of trees and tears
```

The Oak   *Silver Duir*

Gifts
The great English oak, prized for its strength and versatility has been the traditional timber in Britain for making furniture, doors, house structure, and shipbuilding for centuries. Many early Christian chapels were made of oak. Oak bark is used for tanning leather. Oak barrels are used for maturing wine, brandy, and whiskey and oak chippings are excellent for smoking kippers.

Remedies
The oils of this plant used in aromatherapy are extremely powerful and have been used for over a thousand years in helping reverse memory loss and those who have Alzheimer's. Interestingly the tea has been called the 'thinkers tea' as it stimulates the brain and helps with depression.

Wildlife
In the UK, oaks support more species of wildlife than any other tree. Two hundred and eighty species of insects have been found in its canopy. The holes, crannies and bark are homes for owls, bats and insects. Rotting oakwood provides protection and food for stag beetles and their larvae. Deer, badgers and pigs enjoy acorns that are produced once the tree has reached between 30 and 40 years old.

Folklore and Myth   Tree of Endurance and Triumph
The oak was sacred to the Druids whose name derived from their name for oak 'druir', which also means door. Oaks were the doorway to wisdom and strength. Carrying a small talisman of oak in your pocket is said to give you the strength to carry on in adversity.

Oaks were associated with Zeus, Thor, and Jupiter - the gods of thunder. Oaks are more likely than any other tree to be struck by lightning and were connected to rainfall. Paintings that include oak symbolise spiritual nourishment. The oak was a favourite in William Morris's designs.

Celtic Birth Sign: June through July
Oak babies are considered to have the highest form of creativity. They have empathy and understanding and are giving and nurturing. They enjoy being helpful and stand up for the underdog. They love the sense of family and ancestry.

Time for change, each a King for half a
        year.
The Oak and Holly share this role as
        natures seer.

Thyme *Thymus*

Gifts
Thyme is a wonderful aromatic cooking herb that has both antibacterial and anti-fungal properties. Place some of the crushed thyme leaves around the house to frighten off mice and other pests.

Remedies and Recipes
Use thyme in your food instead of salt and this will lower your blood pressure and cholesterol. Making a tea with thyme is excellent for sore throats and colds.

To release the essential oils of the plant, pick and rub them between your hands. The little globules of oil are secreted on the underside of the leaves. The oil is called thymol and contains copper, iron and vitamins C and A. This essential oil when massaged onto the skin scares away the mosquitoes. Thyme oil is very good for treating acne and bronchitis because of its antibacterial signature. We still use thymol in cough sweets today as an effective suppressant.

Roast root vegetables in oil, white-wine vinegar, maple syrup and thyme. Lentils with spinach and thyme make a warming dish. Lemon and thyme also work well together

Folklore and Myth   *element of water*
'Thumus' is ancient Greek for courage and thyme tea was drunk by Highlanders for courage before a battle. An embroidered token of a bee landing on the flower of thyme was given to knights returning from a successful war in recognition of their triumph. Pliny said that "Thyme scares away all venomous creatures".

Fairies have also been linked with thyme over the centuries. In Shakespeare's 'Midsummer Night's Dream' when Oberon, King of the fairies wants to place a love charm on Titania's eyelids whilst she sleeps, he begins,
"I know a bank where the wild thyme blows, where oxlips grow and violets nod their heads, canopied with luscious honeysuckle interspersed with sweet-smelling ramblers and wild roses."
Shakespeare - Oberon 'Mid-Summer Nights Dream'

If you bring thyme into your home you are bringing in the fairies - beware.

Wildlife
Pollinating insects love the flowers of Thyme

Thyme and Basil Pesto.
Wonderful with fish meat or poultry.

Ingredients
170 g fresh parsley
170 g fresh thyme leaves or 1 tablespoon dried,
170 g grated Parmesan
170 g toasted pine nuts or walnuts
2 garlic cloves
170 g olive oil

Finely chop ingredients and place in your processor.
With machine running, gradually add the olive oil
and continue mixing until fairly smooth.
Season to taste with salt and pepper.

St. John's Wort   *hypericum Perforatum*

Gifts

Worldwide, many millions have been made from this plant's gifts. It is non-addictive giving relief from a slightly low mood, winter blues or mild anxiety. It is also being studied for its ability to lessen certain side effects of cancer treatment.

Warning: this must never be used in conjunction with other medicines as the interaction can be very unstable. France has banned its use in products.

St. John's Wort Tea:
Steep 2-3 teaspoons of fresh flowers in hot water for 4 minutes.
Strain out the flowers before drinking. This gives a delightful
lemon-fresh taste. It lifts a low mood if the oil is taken - best
bought in tablet form from sustainable sources.
Identification: hold a leaf up to the light to spot the tiny holes that
contain the oil, or you can squeeze a bud and see the red stain it
leaves on your skin. The deep-red buds start to open into bright
yellow flowers.

It is found more commonly growing in hedgerows and on waste
land. Quite poisonous to livestock.

Remedies
The gleaming bright yellow flowers, red buds and dark leaves
are harvested from June to September. The quick drying process
collects the delicate oil from the glands. This is taken by
millions of people all over the world for anxiety and depression.

Folklore and Myth
Tread on St. John's Wort at your peril. You will be stolen by a faerie
horse.

The plant was used as a tea to increase romance and part of the
plant hung over beds to encourage longevity. It was
dedicated to St. John the Baptist as it bleeds red on his day in June,
the day that John the Baptist was beheaded. It blooms on the solstice and the five petals symbolise a halo of light.

Burn the plant at the Midsummer Fire Festival or take the flowers
through the smoke to ward off ghosts and evil spirits. Bring flowers
into the house on Midsummer's Day to protect the household from
misfortunes, evil spirits, the evil eye, illness and fire. It was
recognised in the same way in China, Greece and Rome, with the
same traditions and uses.

Valerian *Valeriana officinalis*

Gifts
Wild valerian *Valeriana officinalis* is not to be confused with red valerian *Centranthus ruber* a naturalised Mediterranean plant, as this plant does not have any medicinal value.

Wild valerian grows to a height of 1.5 m and has pinky-white flowers and smells sweet. In medieval times it was known as All Heal. You can harvest this root after the first frost in autumn but make sure that the day following the frost is warm to help it dry out.

Remedies and Recipes
The root of this plant has been recognised for thousands of years to help with the quality of sleep and the benefit and relief that it gives for restless leg syndrome and calming nerves. Its soothing effect on the central nervous system is also beneficial for those suffering from Parkinson's disease. Taking this herb helps with Alzheimer's and multiple sclerosis. It calms those with anxiety as it works to keep the neurotransmitters healthy.

Making tea:
The root needs to be cut and dried before being used as a tea. Use one teaspoonful of valerian root three times a day in water.

This herb doesn't have the side effects associated with sleeping pills taken every day. However, never indulge yourself with too many herbal remedies. Valerian in particular is best taken over a short period of time. It is wise not to take valerian in combination with other sleep-inducing pills or medicines. Do not drink alcohol at the same time as taking valerian.

Wildlife
The flowers are delicate and sweet-smelling and attractive to bees and hoverflies. Butterflies also enjoy its nectar. However, the root has a distinctly heavy, strong earthy smell and traditionally attracts rats and cats. The Pied Piper of Hamelin is said to have used its roots to attract the rats out of Hamelin.

Folklore and Myth   *element of air*

This plant is supposed to increase psychic perception and it has
been used for its aphrodisiac properties. Try carrying a sprig
of valerian with you; the scent is believed to attract lovers. In
the books of Harry Potter it was mentioned many times. Hagrid
grew it in his garden.

The Holly *Tinne*

Gifts

We become so aware of holly at Christmas time with its lovely red berries. However, the Holly King is believed to be in charge of the six months of the waning year from Midsummer's day to winter solstice. The leaves were often used as good winter fodder.

The beautiful white wood was chosen to make horse whips as the holly is said to have the element of control. It is also used for marquetry, making tool handles and chess pieces.

Planted near to a house it is said to act as a lightning conductor.

Wildlife

The winter visitors, fieldfare and redwing, love the berries.

Folklore and Myth   Tree of the Waning Year

The Holly wears the crown,
One King dies, another is born,

The waning of the year,
Sir Gawain and the Green Knight,
One carries an oak club, the other a bough of holly.
A holly wreath adorns an oak door, as symbolism of the whole year.
As light decreases, we have more time to see the moon.

The Holly is a symbol of the crown of thorns and Christ's suffering. It is also used as a sign of rebirth. At Christmas time we bring green boughs of Holly into the house, it is said to protect us and remind us of the return of light and life to come. When you see holly in a painting its secret meaning is of domestic happiness.

Celtic Birth Sign: July through August

The holly births are often seen as regal and leaders in their field as they accept challenges and enjoy sorting out problems. They are ambitious and frequently successful in what they do. They are kind, confident and compassionate and keen to do a good job. Look out though as, if not challenged by their work, they can become rather diffident and lazy.

'Blow, blow, thou winter wind,
Thou art not so unkind
As man's ingratitude;
Thy tooth is not so keen

Although thy breath be rude.
Heigh-ho! sing, heigh-ho! unto the green holly:
Most friendship is feigning, most loving mere folly:
Then, heigh-ho, the holly, !his life is most jolly.'

Shakespeare 'As You Like It'

Self Heal *Prunella Vulgarus*

Gifts
You will find this plant amongst short turf on farmland, verges, or gardens that haven't been treated with chemicals. It creeps along the ground keeping a low profile, however, the bees and wasps find it easily, enjoying the nectar. It blooms from June to October, showing little groups of flowers with a deep mauve hood and a lighter coloured tongue. The plant doesn't have a smell but has a square stem similar to mint. It is a member of the dead nettle group or Lamium family.

Recipes and Remedies
This plant is used as an anti-inflammatory; all parts of this plant are edible. Use the leaves and flowers raw in salads, or dried as a tea infusion, it can reduce inflammation and boost the immune system.

It is known to ease the pain of colitis and all sores around the mouth including gingivitis. It is said that it can return thyroid function to normal as it is an amphoteric thyroid herb. Plus it has been acknowledged to help with symptoms of cancer.

It is a wonderful salve for cuts and scratches. Gently rub on your skin for UV protection.

Folklore and Myth
Harvest the plant at night during the dark phase of the moon, preferably when the Dog Star, or by another name, Sirius is rising. The Druids used a sickle to harvest it and then held the cutting aloft with the left hand. After this, thanks should be said. Separate into flowers, leaves, and stems for drying purposes. This plant has so many healing properties, so why not pick with ceremony.

Sense and Self

Sensitive to a look,
Or spider touching with one leg,
Rhythmic sighs, our breath flows to and fro
with waves of life-inspiring thoughts.
Trails of desire,
Needs that try to hide are caught
in dark pools that lower the stranger's eyes
Unwillingly sent, too late the message flies
The soul is bought in quiet ascent.

Sage *Salvere - meaning: to be saved*

Gifts
Sage is a beautiful plant to grow as a herb and also looks good in a border. The leaves are distinctively soft and their colour is light greyish green or purple. The spike flowers come in spring and are in shades of dark blue. The smell from this plant is very distinctive and is used all over the world in flavouring food.

Try tearing the sage leaves into pieces and rubbing them on to your face for a wonderful softening, plumping effect. Use instead of serum.

Recipes and Remedies
Sage is said to stimulate and enhance memory recall. It has been used for thousands of years for this purpose, so if you are struggling for words or can't recall names just try adding sage to your daily diet and watch the improvement in your concentration. It is also beneficial in decreasing hot flushes during menopause.

The Arabian healers were convinced that eating sage gave them immortality. There are others such as the Romans and the Greeks who knew the value of this herb and would have celebrations in its honour.

There are certain food combinations that are really superb. Sage is wonderful both with vegetarian food and with meat. It goes well with white beans, apple and pineapple, infuse it in honey, or add to pesto. It partners with fatty/oily foods. Try an omelette with sage, or add some of the leaves inside a trout. If you eat meat it goes well with pork or beef, but best perhaps with chicken or turkey. If you require the flavour to be strong put the sage in the beginning of your cooking. Add towards the end if you require a somewhat more delicate flavour.

Chop the sage leaves and mix with butter to add to your pasta dish. Try adding some to a cheese sandwich - yum!

The oils of this plant used in aromatherapy are extremely powerful and have been used for over a thousand years in helping reverse memory loss and those who have Alzheimer's. Interestingly the tea has been called the 'thinkers tea' as it stimulates the brain and helps with depression.

Folklore and Myth   *The element of air*

Grow sage in your garden and it ensures the wife therein is well and feeling good. When taken it is said to help with grief when someone dear to you has died.

Smudging sage has been used by witches to clear away evil spirits. To smudge, burn a tight bundle of dried sage; and as it smoulders waft the smoke into all corners through the house or around the person who is suffering, to chase bad spirits away. If you have a dilemma then burning sage helps with your decision making.

German Chamomile and Russian Chamomile
Matricaria chamomilla recutita

Gifts
Sweet chamomile, the therapeutic nature of this plant, rich with essential oils, is known world-wide. The plant and flowers are used as an anti-inflammatory. It is used as a carminative, calming nerves towards sleep.

Remedies
Egyptians loved the medicinal qualities of this herb, so much so that they considered it was a reflection of their Sun God Re. The Anglo Saxons used this herb for calming skin eruptions, as a protection against disease and for its sleep-inducing powers. The Greeks and Romans also used the calming quality of this herb for skin problems and irritations

Chamomile cream soothes the pain of shingles and calms the skin. A mixture of chamomile and cold water is soothing for mouth and throat, cough and colds. The oil is used in cosmetics and shampoo for brightening hair colour. Chamomile tea has a wonderful light fruity flavour and scent. Taken just before bedtime it helps you to have a good nights sleep.

Folklore and Story   *The element of water*
In the book called Peter Rabbit, by Beatrice Potter, Peter's mother gave him a cup of chamomile tea for his nerves and tummy ache after his adventures in Mr. McGregor's garden.

It has the power of nurture and love, beauty and calm, meditation and release, protection and new beginning.

'Though the chamomile, the more it is trodden on the faster it grows, yet youth, the more it is wasted the sooner it wears.'
                    Shakespeare 'King Henry IV Part 1', Act II, Scene 4

Chamomile Skin Cream

1. Take a chamomile tea bag, or dried flowers
2. Blend with almond or coconut oil, lavender flowers.
3. Cook in a slow cooker for 8 hours on low.
4. Leave for 16 hours.
5. Combine beeswax with the contents in a pre-heated bowl.
6. Place in a bain marie, water simmering.
7. Whisk and add drop by drop of tepid water till thick and creamy.
8. Pour into jars.

Wonderfully hydrating healing cream, leaving the skin in beautiful condition.

```
Chamomile tea is made. Taste
The sleep that comes as eye lids droop,
Your bed awaits, your place.
Retreat and rest, the night awaits
Time to sigh,sleep,turn,yawn,
Good night.
```

Burdock   *actium lappa*

Gifts
An enormous plant that can grow to 2m (6 – 9 feet) or more. The plant is edible and also medicinal. Each part has its uses: leaves, seeds and root. It flowers from July to September. You will find it growing wild in hedgerows or by the sides of fields. It is the root that is mostly used medicinally so growing this amazing plant in light soil is best for harvesting. The root extends to 60 cms (2 feet) over the course of the growing season. The seed pods have given us so much - the principle of hook and eye, plus the idea of velcro.

Wildlife
This herb is very attractive to pollinators, bees, wasps and butterflies. Inside the seed head, the larvae of the burdock seed moth can be found. The root is eaten by the larvae of the ghost moth (*Hepialus humuli*). It is called ghost moth as the white males fly together at dusk to entice the female moths. They fall and rise in a display. It can take two winters before the larvae turns into moths .

Remedies and Recipes
If you suffer from skin complaints you can apply a leaf or the anti-inflammatory antibacterial root sap directly on the skin by cutting a section of the root and peeling off the outer skin before applying. Boil the leaves and add the cooking water to your bath. This soothes and softens irritated skin for example chickenpox. A solution of burdock gives hair a shiny appearance when used as a last rinse.

For a tea, use the core of the root, make peelings with your potato peeler and let them dry out overnight. This is a blood-purifying, gut-improving, skin-softening, hair-stimulating drink. It is found to attack tumours as it promotes health in the pancreas. Healthy hair and skin and gut, what could be better! Plus it increases your sex drive!
Don't take it if you are pregnant. Don't give it to children either. If you are not sure, ask your doctor.

If you are camping, try wrapping your food in three layers of burdock leaves instead of tinfoil. You could try cleaning the whole root and cooking it in soup sliced in small rounds. If you are cooking the root it is best to leave it to soak overnight to take away some of the bitterness. The root (gobo) and young leaves are a common food in Japan.

Folklore and Myth

The element of air

The symbolism of this plant can be seen woven into Turkish kilims (a woven carpet), as it is said that burdock wards off the evil eye and brings abundance and flowers. These carpets have been made for centuries. Burdock was woven into hair and hung over doorways or on the roof in medieval times to ward off evil spirits.

Borage *Borago officinalis*

Gifts
This particularly hairy plant seems to come from nothing each year.
The first signs of a little spindly sprout grows in the spring, eventually
reaching a height of 60-100 cms. By June or July the exquisite purple/blue
star-shaped flowers hang down from their stems. Perhaps best fitting into
a corner of the herb garden. It has many uses as both the leaves and
flowers are edible. It can be used to decorate a salad dish or added to your
drinks. Planted in a vegetable garden, it is a good companion to tomatoes
apparently improving the flavour.

Recipes and Remedies
Borage seed oil can be applied to skin or hair to improve condition.
Borage oil should be diluted with a carrier oil if taken to improve skin
structure. It can help with inflammation as it prevents cell damage.
Borage oil dilates the blood vessels; this improves circulation and can
help with acne and hot flushes.

Taking borage for a few months regularly can reduce rheumatoid
arthritis. Try grinding up the leaves for an herbal tea. The crunchy hairy
leaves taste a little like cucumber. Do not use if you suffer from epilepsy.

Wildlife
If grown near to other plants it can prevent disease or pests. Bees love the
flowers as do hover flies. Butterflies are also attracted to the flowers and you
may find the little green eggs of the painted lady butterfly.

Folklore and Myth *The element of air*
Borage symbolises bravery. The Celts and Romans would drink wine with
borage flowers just before going into battle to give them courage.
Flowers embroidered on the scarves of medieval knights have been
identified as borage. If you would like a proposal of marriage, try giving
your lover a cup of borage tea.

Borage oil was often put in the four corners of a room to bring harmony
into the home. It was also used to clean the floor, making the room
smell fresh.

In the 17th century motifs of flowers and herbs were
embroidered on to their fashionable jackets, each design was
unique. Borage was one of the most common plants to be used,
entwining among the strawberries, pansies, honeysuckle etc.
Unusually, two jackets with exactly the same design can be seen in
the fashion museum in Bath and in the Burrell collection in Glasgow.

Lavender *Lavandula*

Gifts

This wonderful fragrant herb which came originally from the Mediterranean, is used widely in gardens creating beautiful drifts of colour. The perfume follows you around the paths giving a sense of purity and grace, serenity and calmness. A wonderful massage or bath oil. Lavender sachets can be made and put under pillows to induce sleep or to perfume and freshen drawers and rooms.

To grow your own lavender you need to plant in full sun and to have dry well-drained soil. The silver-grey leaf and purple flowers of lavender planted alongside roses add perfumes right through from spring to the end of autumn.

Four thieves vinegar.
A jar of apple cider vinegar
Garlic cloves
Rosemary, lavender, sage, thyme
Black peppercorn
Camphor dissolved in spirit,
Bruised cloves

Put all these ingredients together and leave for 4-6 weeks and then strain. Use against insects, negativity and nightmares, and for protection.

The story behind the name:

This secret recipe was said to have been used by four Marseilles thieves entering the houses of plague victims at the time of the Black Death. As plague-carrying fleas were repelled, they were protected.

Remedies
The lavender oil is used to lift mood and soothe anxious stomach disorders and helps heal headaches. Lavender water was considered to cure migraines. This was made from gin or brandy combined with lavender.

A powerful antiseptic, it helps to heal wounds and for thinning hair, rub lavender oil onto your head to encourage new growth.

Combined with rosemary it is said that the perfume increases brain power and fertility.

Folklore and Myth
The element of air

'Here's flowers for you;
Hot lavender, mints, savoury, marjoram;
The marigold, that goes to bed wi' the sun
And with him rises weeping: these are flowers
Of middle summer, and I think they are given
To men of middle age.'

              Shakespeare 'A Winters Tale' Act 4 Scene 4 Line 122

Confusing messages appear in old manuscripts and tales. Some talk of love and lavender, the one entwined with the other. If lavender is left under a pillow it is said to create passion in a marriage. Alternatively, it is said, a young girl wearing the scent of lavender would ward off any potential approach from young men.

It was believed that the plant guarded against cruelty. Used in paintings it holds a meaning of distrust.

So many mixed messages from a single plant.

'As Rosemary is to the spirit so Lavender is for the soul'
Anon.

Blackberry   *Rubus aboriginum*

Gifts
The humble bramble 'walks' through the woods carefully placing a 'tentacle' into the earth. This soon entwines into tangled, prickly, vigorous growth.

A blackberry is in fact not a berry but rather they are called drupelets similar to the raspberry.

Recipes and Remedies
Family fun, going to gather the fruit in autumn as winter approaches with its sleepiness and dreams. Dogs too seem to enjoy picking and eating the fruit from the lower branches.

High in vitamin C, the fruit helps the immune system against colds. It can be made into drinks, pies, and jellies, and can be used along with the stems and leaves as hair and fabric dye. Mouth sores and bleeding gums can be eased by chewing the leaves or using them to make a tea.

Wildlife
Bramble thickets protect nests and fledglings, for example the long-tailed tit, as well as small mammals. The flowers being simple and open are a wonderful source of nectar for pollinators. Harvest mice eat the new young leaves. Brambles also shield young trees from being grazed by deer. Badgers enjoy fallen fruit along with the foxes and voles. So the blackberry bush is a haven for many birds, mammals, and insects.

Folklore and Myth
The blackberry in paintings is often used as an allegory for spiritual ignorance or neglect.

It is said that the Devil or Lucifer was thrown out of heaven on September 30th and landed in a blackberry bush. Every year the devil returns on this date and is said to spit on the fruit turning it black and bitter, so forget harvesting the fruit after this date!

Bramble trips and stops you in your tracks
Catches your coat and scratches your skin,
The fruit is ripe and now we must begin.

We picked to fill our cans and jars
Our blue-black fingers marked with blood and stain,
Around our mouths a thunder cloud with tell tale
sign plain to all that fruit is some for now and
others gain
From cooking apples swelled by autumn rain
To make a crumble feast with custard once again.

Beech *Fagus Sylvatica Pulpuria*

Gifts
Considered the Queen of the forest, the wonderful colours of the leaves and the beautiful shape of the fully grown tree with its smooth bark gives a feeling of strength and restful beauty. The beech gives us attractive timber used in making furniture such as chairs, tool handles, stocks for rifles, and veneer. The tree can live to 300 years and if coppiced can live for 1000 years. The Romans introduced the tree to Scotland and from the timber they manufactured drinking bowls. In the 19th century the oil from beech was used for cooking and for fuel to light lamps. The tar from the timber was used to make creosote. Many couples from long ago have carved their initials into beech tree bark, allowing us to dwell on untold stories.

Wildlife
With a thick canopy in Summer, beech trees provide a habitat for many butterflies and moths and their young, for example the Buff Tip moth caterpillars who munch happily through the leaves. Badgers, deer, mice and squirrels, hedgehogs and jays and many other birds enjoy the leaves and mast of beech trees. From April to July squirrels like to strip the bark to enjoy the sap.

Remedies and Recipes
The bark has an astringent effect and has been used for piles, boils, and other skin conditions. An old Indian recipe for beech tea, it has been said, gives you good health. To make beech tea, pick 5 grammes of dried beech leaves found on hedges in the winter and steep them in 500 ml of boiling water for 25 minutes, a delicious drink, but warning, do not try this if you are pregnant.

Young beech leaves are good with salad, they have a taste similar to grapes or sorrel, delicious with mackerel. Beech nuts are very tasty when roasted but eat too many and they can have a poisonous effect on some people.

A fairly intense liqueur called Noyau, originating in the Chilterns, is made from the beech leaves. You can find it for sale in various parts of the country, particularly in Cornwall. It tastes a little oily, rather like sake. Originally made from the kernel of the beech nut, it is now made from the very young bright green Spring leaves. If you want to make your own, steep a litre of the young leaves in a 750ml of gin for two weeks and then add 250ml each of brandy, water and sugar. Leave this to mature for two more weeks. Well worth a try.

Folklore
Beech symbolises wisdom in your writings and creativity. It is a tree full of wishes. Take a branch and write your wish on it, then stick it deep into the ground by the tree and your message will go to the Fairy Queen who may grant your wish to you. A piece of the beech tree kept in your pocket will give you confidence, success and improve your luck. A forked twig or branch can be used as a diving rod.

The scent of oil of beech induces feelings of hope. Used as a massage oil it is supposed to increase tolerance and empathy. You can use a branch of the beech as a wand to open understanding between adversaries.

The beech represents the death or end of something and the beginning of the next chapter. It challenges you to brave the future and to use your experience to discover knowledge of what is yet unknown. Try choosing a space within a beech wood, a sunny glade, and then make a ritual that you can perform there every time you visit. This allows you to see the bigger picture of your place in the world, your future, your life. If you make a powder of the bark and place it in one of your shoes, you will always walk towards your fortune. It is said that if you prepare yourself for opportunities, then you create opportunities.

Vervain *verbena officianalis*

Gifts
Vervain grows wild on rough grasslands, coastal cliffs and likes free-draining soil. The showy erect stems with small clusters of little purple flowers, vervain reminds me of a candelabra. Rather similar in some instances to the Menorah .

Wild Life
Insects, especially honey bees, are attracted to this plant for nectar.

Recipes and Remedies
Vervain brings calm and relaxation after mental stress, insomnia and over-exertion. It nourishes the nervous system over time. It is used for those suffering from depression and anxiety. It is also used for gout, kidney stones and headache. Powered dried flowers were also used to staunch nose bleeds.

Folklore and Myth
Vervain was considered a sacred magical plant by the Romans and Druids. The ancient Egyptian story is that the goddess Isis wept as she gathered her son's body parts, which had been widely distributed by her jealous brother Seth. Where her tears fell, vervain grew and so it was known as 'Tears of Isis'. The blossom of vervain is also found on the cimaruta, an Italian folk charm hung on babies' beds to ward off the evil eye. The design, based on a sprig of rue, was used as a part of an amulet. Accredited with mighty powers of protection, worn around the neck it wards off headaches and is said to bring help when you most need it.

Plant vervain in the garden to protect your house from bad weather. Vervain tea protects you from vampires.

There are many names for vervain, here are three of them:
holy cross, mosquito plant and wild hyssop.

The Hazel   *Coll*

Gifts
Plaited hazel strips are wound round the rim of new coracles.
Also used in weaving baskets, hurdles and wattle. The charcoal made from
the branches makes crayons and gun powder. The nuts, delicious to eat, are
known to be brain food as apparently, they give double the protein of eggs
for the same weight, increasing creativity. When ground into flour, it makes
delicious bread and cakes.

Remedies
A magical tree, full of medicinal goodness. The nuts are full of calcium,
vitamin E, magnesium and potassium. Ground down with added honey and
water cures coughs. The witch hazel is a medicinal astringent made from the
leaves and bark of the witch hazel. Tea made from the tree, treats varicose
veins, fevers, circulatory problems and diarrhoea.

Wildlife
The nuts are food for both of our squirrel species red and grey. They
are also much loved by the dormouse and wood mice. You can tell when
a dormouse has been visiting by the scratching at the base of the trunks.
The woodpecker and wood pigeons amongst others enjoy visiting the
hazelnuts. Also there are many kinds of moth and the fritillary butterfly
make the hazel their home.

Folklore and Myth   Tree of Wisdom and Immortality
The hazel is mentioned in Shakespeare, Grim's fairy tales and Greek
mythology. Wisdom comes from walking sticks made of hazel, protecting
against evil spirits.The hazel awakens inner intuition and insight, stimulates
poetic and artistic skills and calms passions. A fishing rod made from hazel
gives the fisherman knowledge of where best to fish. The hazel fork is used as
a divining rod.

Eating the nuts can induce visions leading to greater awareness. Hazelnuts
can be carried as charms, warding off rheumatism and lumbago.

Celtic Birth Sign: August through September
These folk are quiet and although intelligent and have ideas that they work
through right to the last detail, it is not something that they boast about. They
are friendly and generous people. They are faithful partners, although can be
moody if disappointed. Although usually successful they are not fond of
luxury. They are very adaptable to situations and naturally smart.

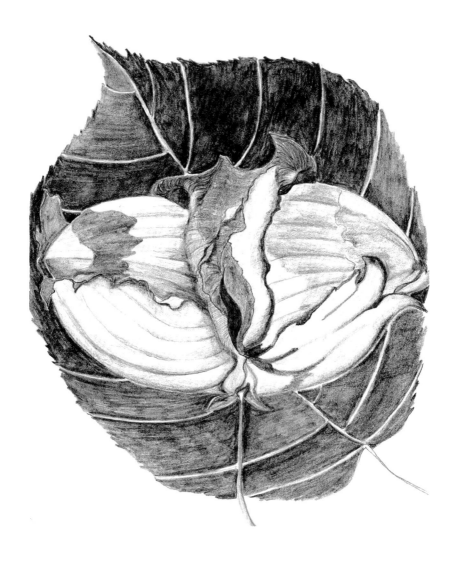

Her chariot is an empty hazelnut
Made by the joiner squirrel or old grub,
Time out o'mind the fairies' coachmakers.'
      Shakespeare: Romeo and Juliet Act 1 scene 4.

The Vine *vīnea*

Gifts
Grapevines are grown successfully in Britain producing award-winning sparkling wine. The vines are excellent for covering pergolas or trellis work giving colour, greenery, and of course lovely grapes. Grapevines can last for up to 30 years if cared for appropriately.

Grapes have been highly valued for thousands of years. The vines were brought into Britain in AD43 by the Romans. There is evidence that they used the wine to add to their drinking water as it probably helped to purify the water and disguise the taste.

Remedies
Red grapes are full of antihistamine and are known to have anti-inflammatory properties. The skin of the red grape contains more antioxidants than the green. These are excellent for a variety of complaints of the digestive system and helps with cancers of breast and liver. Grape juice, lemon juice and a spoonful of honey - a great way to treat coughs.

Folklore and Myth
The grape is known for its fertility and for its magic which is associated with the Roman god Bacchus or Greek god Dionysus. The Greek cult worshipped Dionysus by drinking wine and dancing to a rhythmic beat until, in a trance-like state, they claimed to be filled with the god's spirit. Their unconscious minds in a state of euphoria. In Greek mythology Dionysus fell in love with the beautiful satyr called Ampelos who was pretty reckless and decided to ride a wild bull. He was tossed off his back and gored to death. Dionysus in his grief turned him into the first grapevine.

In Jewish mythology, it was thought that Eve ate grapes rather than an apple. The Bible referred to grapes when Moses sent two men out to find food, they came back with an enormous bunch of grapes carried between them. The vine is always assoicated with abundance and plenty.

In art it symbolises eternity and connectivity as the spiral tendrils twist and turn around their support, drawing everything together.

Celtic Birth Sign: Through September
Those born at this time are charming but fairly indecisive as they can see both sides of an argument. They do know about art and music and enjoy a little luxury. They love food and wine. They have style and can turn anything into something beautiful. They are always there for you.

Dancing to the rhythmn of
fruit and vine,
Enjoy the wine.

The Ivy *Gort* *Hedera Helix*

Gifts
The mysterious ivy creeps and climbs forming shelter for our wildlife in its dark interiors. The clinging tentacles do no harm to trees or buildings, in fact ivy can give insulation and protect from rain damage. However, eventually, it can become too heavy for tree branches, and ivy roots can work their way into aging delapidated stone work, pushing the cracks further apart.

In Roman and Greek times the crown of ivy was a sign of achievement in both intellectual and athletic fields. It is also a sign of fidelity, which is probably where the tradition of having ivy in the bouquet of a bride or as part of the table decorations comes from. The evergreen of holly and ivy at Christmas time is used to celebrate that there is life in the darkest months.

Wildlife
The ivy provides habitat and protection for a great variety of animals. Squirrels, owls, smaller birds and insects find it a great place to hibernate, roost, nest, and feed. The flowers are much loved by hoverflies, bees and wasps. At night, it attracts the lovely swallow-tail moth with its delicate light-green wings. A relatively new arrival in the UK is the ivy bee that forages only among the flowers in September. It is a solitary bee that burrows into soft sandy banks. It has reached southern England and parts of Wales and was first sited in 2001.

Folklore and Myth   The tree of resurrection
Ivy has always been associated with drunkenness as crowns of ivy were thought to prevent hangovers. Bacchus/Dionysus are always portrayed wearing a wreath of ivy. Herbalists use ivy as part of a medicine for congestion and chronic bronchial problems. The berries are toxic and are not to be eaten. The ivy that you see in paintings is a symbol of fidelity.

Celtic Birth Sign: Through October
Those born at this time are known to be very giving, understanding often shy but charismatic. They help others who need support. They have great compassion and a sharp intellect. They withstand trouble and go through life with grace and perseverance. They can be delightful in social situations. They also have great faith during tough times.

Ivy tendrils cling to safety.
The mysterious dark hides
Secret sleeping life within.

Fennel *foeniculum vulgare*

Gifts

Fennel with its high fibre and potassium has much to give us. Full of vitamins, fennel prevents damage to cells. This special plant fights and slows the ageing process.

Around 492 BC the Greek army won an important battle against the Persians in an area where wild fennel grows abundantly. A young soldier ran 42 kilometres from Marathon to Athens to tell the news of the victory. Thus the name of the long-distance run, marathon. The name for fennel in Greece is maratho which means literally, fennel field. Roman soldiers chewed fennel seeds for courage before going into battle

Remedies and Recipes

Every part of the fennel plant can be eaten and is known to give you strength and longevity.

Adding fennel to your beauty routine:
Make a tea by pouring boiling water onto the leaves and allow this to steep for 10 minutes. Use the water with a little lemon added to tone your face after cleansing, leaving your skin soft and bright.

Myth and Folklore

The stem of the giant fennel was used to make thyrsus wands. These were decorated by ribbons, wrapped in ivy and topped by a pine cone. They symbolised eternal life and fertility. Prometheus used a thyrsus wand to carry the stolen fire he gifted to humankind.

'There's fennel for you, and columbines; there's rue for you, and here's some for me, we may call it herb of grace o' Sundays: O, you must wear your rue with difference'

Shakespeare: Hamlet Act 4 scene 5

Ophelias' mad scene, although maybe she wasn't mad as she hands out flowers with their secret meanings; fennel for flattery, foolishness and maybe for adultery as well.

The Reed *Phragmites australis*

Gifts
The wonderful expanses of reed beds give life and building materials for animals, birds and humans. It is sometimes known as marsh or water elder. The Norfolk reed is used for thatching. Reed beds are excellent for cleaning water from sewage using micro-organisms that live within the root systems.

The long reed stem can be made into paper, mats, boats and baskets. Grind the roots and the saplings into flour, for cereals or dumplings. Boil the leaves and roll into balls for a sweet treat. The flower heads can produce a pale-green dye. Originally the sharp point of the reeds were used for spear heads and part of the reed was used in the mouthpieces of wind instruments.

Wildlife
Many birds love the reed beds as a habitat to produce their young. You will find bittern, reed and sedge warblers, the rare marsh harrier and water rails. Roosting birds can also make the reeds their home. Small mammals enjoy the habitat too such as harvest mice, water voles and water shrews.

Folklore and Myth   Tree of established power, the inquisitor
The reed is certainly not a tree but in the Celtic meaning, any woody plant with roots that are solid, entwined and massed under the earth; were considered to be trees. The Greek god Pan had a musical duel with Apollo to see who could play the sweetest music using the reed. Pan won, Apollo became furious and turned him into half goat half man. The reed in a painting symbolises a voice that yearns to be heard, bending, fragile becoming a consequence of desire.

Celtic Birth Sign: Late October through November
Always looking for the sub-text, what is not said but intimated. They make good historians as they are passionate about a real story, one where they can dig deep to find answers and happenings and reasons why.
They make good journalists, guides, interviewers and film makers. They can manipulate circumstances to their advantage but overall they are honourable, truth seekers and secret keepers.

Moss *Bryophyta*

Gifts

There are many species of moss, most found in dank places. In damp woodland, verdant emerald green moss covers fallen trees, old walls or banks. You can be guided through a forest by moss which grows on the north side of trees. However, care needs to be taken as it can grow where there is standing water so finding north will be more difficult. Used in gardens it is very low maintenance, can soften hard surfaces be planted between stones on a pathway and used to give damp areas a green glow.

Sphagnum moss can be found in temperate rather wet climates in northern areas and in Ireland where the rain invites it to grow profusely. Its beauty comes from the different shades and colours of different species.
It absorbs water like a sponge. Decayed moss or peat is used as fuel, and by gardeners, as it gives nutrition to plants and helps retain water. This is now discouraged as peat bogs are a vulnerable habitat and important carbon sequesters.

Remedies

Sphagnum moss was used historically for nappies, absorbent pads, bandages and sponges. During the First World War, the moss was gathered and used to pack wounds of the soldiers where it absorbed and stemmed the flow of blood and inhibited the growth of bacteria due to its antiseptic and sterile nature.

Wildlife

Moss is an important habitat for invertebrates and therefore attracts birds looking for food.

Folklore and Myth

There are stories of wood folk or moss people that seem to originate from Germany. The folk who live in-between were known as the Moss People, or sometimes wood wives. Unsociable and shy, they are small and grey, often with long hair, they live in the wildness of wood and moorland. They are known to travel quietly, venturing into farms at night to complete outstanding chores, and cure sick animals. In return, bowls of porridge and bread are left outside for them as gifts. However, if they are not rewarded or recognised for their work then they become disruptive to the farmer and bring difficulties into their lives. It is symbolic of money and luck.

A rolling stone gathers no moss

Propagating Moss

A simple method is to take some live moss, and buttermilk, blend it up into a slurry. Then cover any surface where you want moss to grow. Keep it misted until the moss is well established.

```
The Chapel
Blind beauty of sculptured silent stones,
Worn by ancient wind and rain,
Hear their witness of the past.
Leaning on the abbey wall,
A gargoyle's dark and gaping mouth.
With mossy empty breath, gasps.
```

Parsley   *petroselinum crispum*

Gifts
Parsley flavours a meal without having to add salt or sugar, it also aids digestion, is known to be good for the immune system and to promote well-being.

Remedies
Medieval herbalists recommended parsley for upset stomachs. This plant contains vitamin K and one of the highest concentrations of myricetin, a flavonoid, in plants that we know. This has been proven to help prevent skin cancer and diabetes. Apigenin, a natural chemical also found in parsley was shown to decrease the size of a tumour in aggressive breast cancer.

It is also of nutritional benefit to increase bone strength. Those people who have consumed high levels of vitamin K, found in dark-green leafy vegetables, are shown to have fewer bone fractures as it helps the absorption of calcium. Ten sprigs of parsley is an adequate daily dose. Because of the high vitamin K content it is not to be taken at the same time as blood thinners.

Recipes
Parsley is excellent when paired with:
potatoes
tomato-based sauces
poultry
grain salads
seafood
egg dishes
ham

If you enjoy charred steak then have plenty of green vegetables, especially parsley to stop the cancerous effect of eating meat that has been grilled at high temperatures.

Folklore and Myth   *The element of air*
Parsley is a symbol of celebration and carnival. It was thought to remove emotional upsets and clear the air between lovers. It is not easy to germinate so best planted by a female on friday before Easter at noon. The one who cultivates parsley is considered to be the most dominant person in the household.

Vegetarian salad
    12 sprigs of parsley roughly chopped
    half a red onion chopped
    6 cherry tomatoes
    12 olives
    squeezed lemon
    pinch of salt
    add sliced avocado on the top.

You can always add some beans or hard boiled eggs to make a
substantial, healthy and delicious meal.

The Elder *Aeld*

Gifts
This tree has clusters of white flowers and in the autumn red berries. The name comes from Elihorn (meaning fire), the hollow stems of the young branches having been used for blowing on a fire to start a blaze. After the pith had been removed, the tubes were used as pipes, often called the pipe tree. Come children used these tubes to make pop guns.

Remedies and Recipes
The elderberry juice is beneficial for combatting flu, sinus pain, back and leg pain (sciatica), nerve pain and chronic fatigue. It also helps with cancer, sweating, and is a laxative for constipation. It seems to attack various viruses as it builds the immune system.

The white flowers and gooseberries when cooked together make tasty fools, preserves and jam. Elderflower cordial is a delicious drink, light and refreshing. Elder is used to make wine and flavour food, as is much loved by herbalists and chefs.

Wildlife
The elder pests are the soft scale and the aphids that feed voraciously on the leaf leaving honeydew mould. The ladybirds come and predate and in turn they are predated by all manner of birds. A great variety of moths are found on the elder. The flowers attract the pollinators and small mammals, dormice and bank voles enjoy the berries.

Folklore and Myth   The Seeker
This tree is known as the fairy tree. Called Tramman in the Isle of Man where it grows abundantly. In Ireland it is thought to be possessed by fairies or demons. The pan pipes made from this tree are considered to make the shrillest sound of all pipes.

Celtic Birth Sign: November through December
They are freedom lovers and can appear a little wild in comparison to other Celtic signs. They can appear withdrawn and thoughtful with a philosophical bent, although extrovert in nature. They strive to help others and try to be considerate although their brutal honesty can be shared maybe too openly. Can be seen as the outsider or black sheep however they are sincere but need constant challenges.

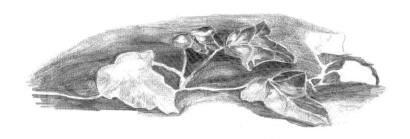

A Walk in the Woods

Walking in the evening's fading light
This wood knows the yearning for what was once, now past.
The fragrance of the earth releases into the night
As the seeds of a thousand trees are cast.

Taking the quiet in my hand,
Breathing the evening air,
A memory stirs and the ache of love
Suddenly leaps and lingers there.

Coloured by distance, a fleeting glance
Of loosely stitched times to have and to hold
As the wind returns and the leaves dance
Together, quicken, spin and fold.

The trees heal this jagged space,
Caressing with outstretched arms.
The sun on the rooftop lies close by
Nature sighs, a note of calm.

Walking in this healing wood, the spirit lifts
In thanks to nature's silent gifts.

INDEX